Alfred's
Easy guitar songs
CLASSIC ROCK

50 HITS OF THE '60s, '70s & '80s

Produced by
Alfred Music
P.O. Box 10003
Van Nuys, CA 91410-0003
alfred.com

Printed in USA.

ISBN-10: 1-4706-3285-3
ISBN-13: 978-1-4706-3285-4

Cover Photos
Gibson Hummingbird courtesy of Gibson Brands • Duesenberg Dragster DC courtesy of Duesenberg Guitars, USA

artist index

contents

TITLE	ARTIST	

STRUM PATTERNS

Below are a number of suggested patterns that may be used while strumming the chords for the songs in this book. Think of these as starting points from which you may embellish, mix up, or create your own patterns.

Note the markings above the staff that indicate the direction of the strums.

⊓ indicates a downstroke

V indicates an upstroke

FINGERPICKING PATTERNS

Here are some fingerpicking patterns that may be used to arpeggiate chords where indicated in this book.
As with the strum patterns, these are starting points from which you may embellish, mix up, or create your own patterns.

Note the fingerings:
p = thumb
i = index finger
m = middle finger
a = ring finger

⊓ indicates a downstroke   ∨ indicates an upstroke

Fingerpicking Pattern #1:

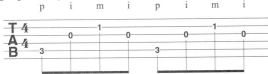

Fingerpicking Pattern #2:

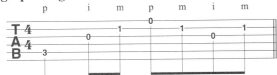

Fingerpicking Pattern #3:

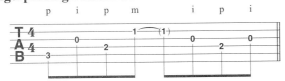

Fingerpicking Pattern #4:

Fingerpicking Pattern #5:

Fingerpicking Pattern #6:

Fingerpicking Pattern #7:

Fingerpicking Pattern #8:

Fingerpicking Pattern #9:

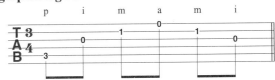

Fingerpicking Pattern #10:

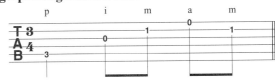

Fingerpicking Pattern #11:

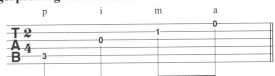

Fingerpicking Pattern #12:

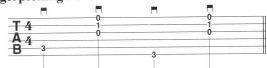

Fingerpicking Pattern #13:

Fingerpicking Pattern #14:

BABY IT'S YOU

Use Suggested Strum Pattern #5
Moderately ♩ = 96

Words and Music by
BURT BACHARACH, MACK DAVID
and BARNEY WILLIAMS

Verse:

1. It's not the way you smile that touched my heart.
2. Is it true what they say about you?

It's not the way you kiss that tears me apart.
They say you'll never ever never be true.

Chorus:

1. Man-y, man-y, man-y nights go by, I sit a-lone at home and cry o-
2. It does-n't mat-ter what they say, I know I'm gon-na love you an-y old way. What

-ver you. What can I do? Don't want no-bod-y, no-bod-y,
can I do with-out you?}

Baby It's You - 2 - 1

BEHIND BLUE EYES

Use Suggested Strum Pattern #6

Moderately ♩ = 120

Words and Music by
PETER TOWNSHEND

Use Suggested Strum Pattern #2

Interlude:

Bridge:

When my fist clench - es, crack it o - pen, be - fore I use___

___ it and lose___ my cool.___ When I smile___ tell___ me some bad___

___ news be - fore I laugh___ and act like a fool.___

And if I swal - low an - y-thing e - vil, put your fin - ger down___ my

25 OR 6 TO 4

Words and Music by
ROBERT LAMM

Use Suggested Strum Pattern #6

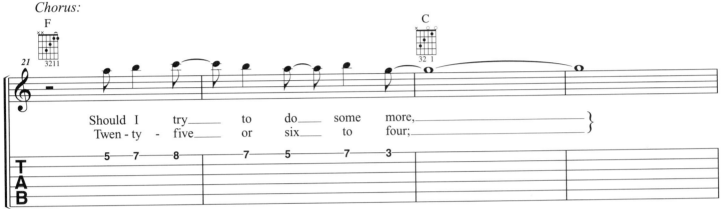

Chorus:

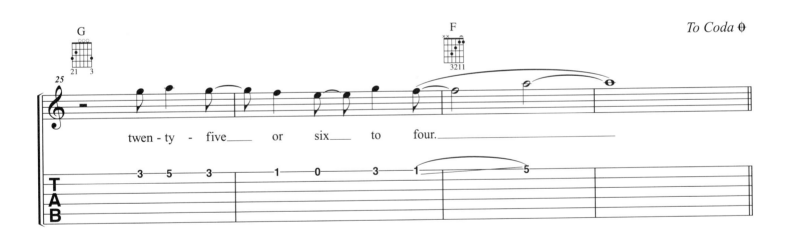

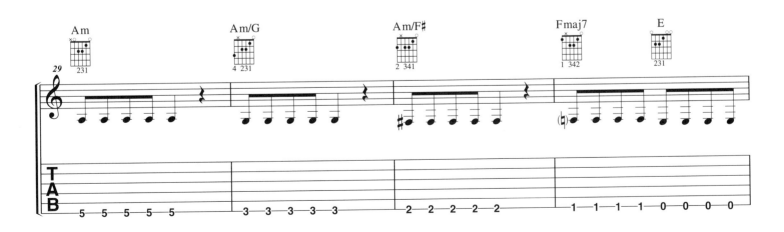

25 or 6 to 4 - 3 - 2

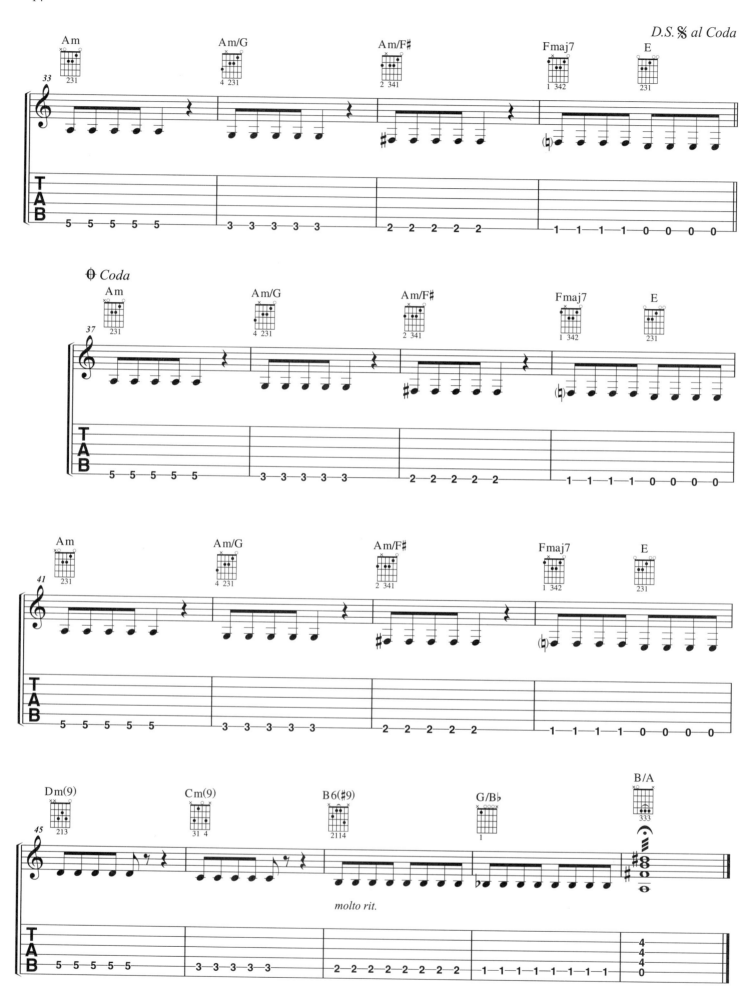

D.S. % al Coda

25 or 6 to 4 - 3 - 3

BORN TO RUN

Words and Music by
BRUCE SPRINGSTEEN

Use Suggested Strum Pattern #1 or #6

Moderately ♩ = 138

Verse 2:
Wendy, let me in, I wanna be your friend,
I want to guard your dreams and visions.
Just wrap your legs 'round these velvet rims
And strap your hands across my engines.
Together we could break this trap,
We'll run 'til we drop, baby, we'll never go back.
Will you walk with me out on the wire,
'Cause, baby, I'm just a scared and lonely rider.
But I gotta find out how it feels,
I want to know if love is wild, girl, I want to know if love is real.
(To Saxophone Solo:)

Verse 3:
The highway's jammed with broken heroes
On a last chance power drive.
Everybody's out on the run tonight but there's no place left to hide.
Together, Wendy, we can live with the sadness,
I'll love you with all the madness in my soul.
Someday, girl, I don't know when, we're gonna get to that place
Where we really want to go and well walk in the sun.
But 'til then, tramps like us, baby, we were born to run.
Ah, honey, tramps like us, baby, we were born to run.
Come on with me, tramps like us, baby, we were born to run.
(To Outro:)

CAN'T YOU SEE

Use Suggested Strum Pattern #4 or
Suggested Fingerpicking Pattern #2

Words and Music by
TOY CALDWELL

Moderately slow ♩ = 84

Can't You See - 3 - 1

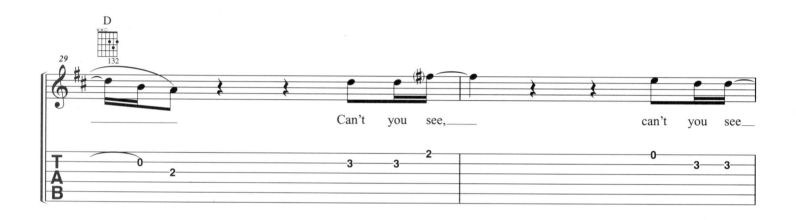

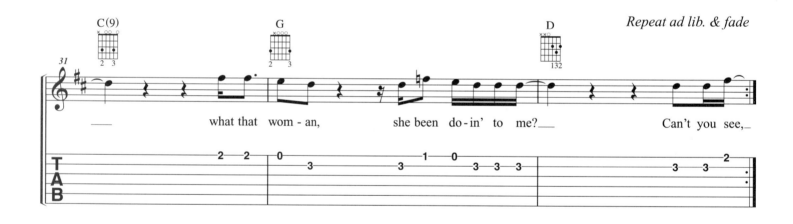

Verse 2:
I'm gonna buy a ticket now,
As far as I can, ain't never comin' back.
Grab me a southbound all the way to Georgia now,
'Til the train, it run out of track.
(To Chorus:)

THE CIRCLE GAME

Use Suggested Fingerpicking Pattern #6

Words and Music by
JONI MITCHELL

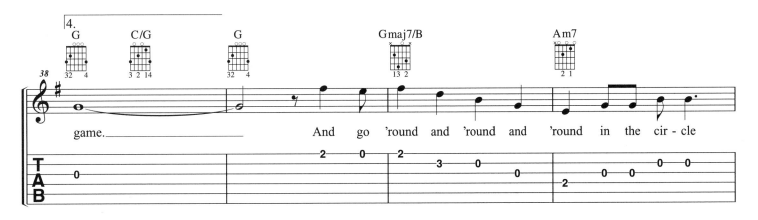

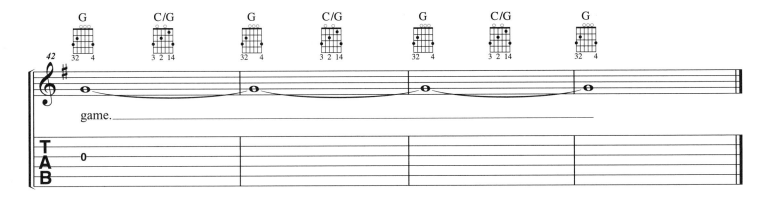

Verse 2:
Then the child moved ten times 'round the seasons
Skated over ten clear, frozen streams
Words like "when you're older" must appease him
And promises of someday make his dreams
(To Chorus:)

Verse 3:
Sixteen springs and sixteen summers gone now
Cartwheels turn to carwheels through the town
And they tell him take your time, it won't be long now
Till you drag your feet to slow the circles down
(To Chorus:)

Verse 4:
So the years spin by and now the boy is twenty
Though his dreams have lost some grandeur coming true
There'll be new dreams, maybe better dreams, and plenty
Before the last revolving year is through
(To Chorus:)

THE CHAIN

Use Suggested Strum Pattern #6

Words and Music by
LINDSEY BUCKINGHAM, CHRISTINE McVIE,
STEVIE NICKS, MICK FLEETWOOD and JOHN McVIE

The Chain - 4 - 1

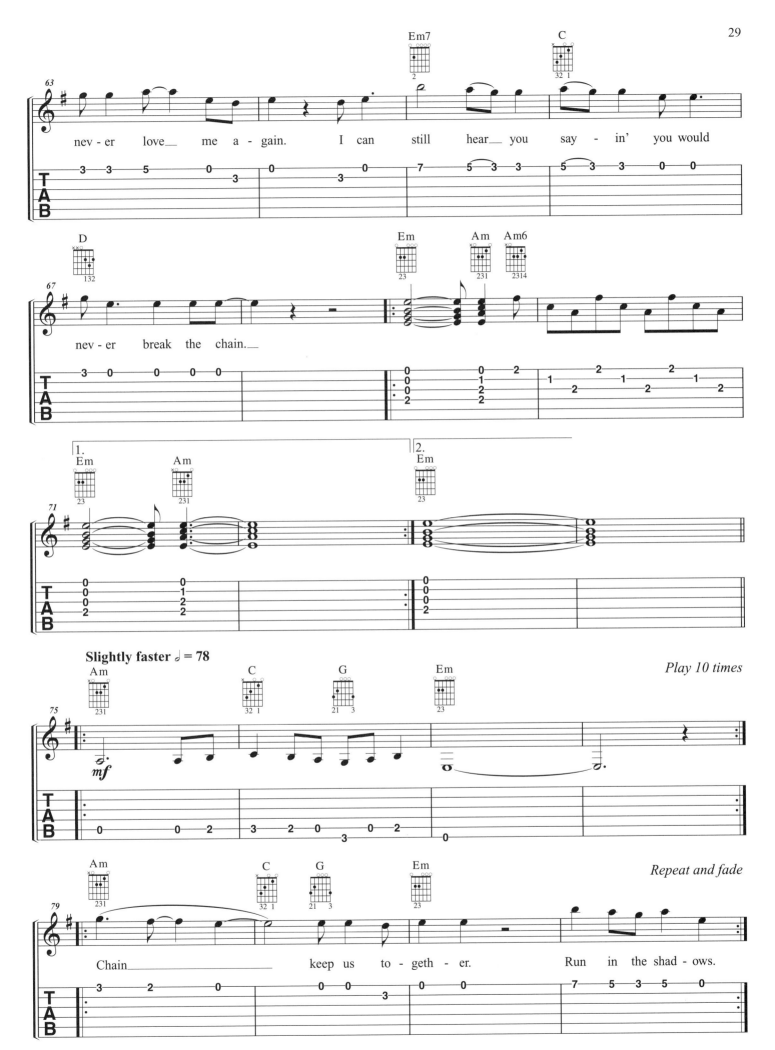

COLOUR MY WORLD

Words and Music by
JAMES PANKOW

Use Suggested Strum Pattern #13
Slowly ♩. = 52

DANCING IN THE DARK

Use Suggested Strum Pattern #1

Moderately fast ♩ = 144

Words and Music by
BRUCE SPRINGSTEEN

Dancing in the Dark - 3 - 1

Verse 2:
Message keeps getting clearer;
Radio's on and I'm moving 'round the place.
I check my look in the mirror;
I wanna change my clothes, my hair, my face.
Man, I ain't getting nowhere just living in a dump like this.
There's something happening somewhere;
Baby, I just know there is.
(To Chorus:)

Verse 3:
Stay on the streets of this town
And they'll be carving you up all right.
They say you got to stay hungry;
Hey, baby, I'm just about starving tonight.
I'm dying for some action;
I'm sick of sitting 'round here trying to write this book.
I need a love reaction;
Come on now, baby, gimme just one look.
(To Chorus:)

DO YOU FEEL LIKE WE DO

Words and Music by
PETER FRAMPTON, JOHN SIOMOS,
RICK WILLIS and MICK GALLAGHER

Use Suggested Strum Pattern #6

Moderately ♩ = 106

Do You Feel Like We Do - 2 - 1

DO YOU WANT TO KNOW A SECRET

**Use Suggested Strum Pattern #4
or Fingerpicking Pattern #4**

Words and Music by
JOHN LENNON and PAUL McCARTNEY

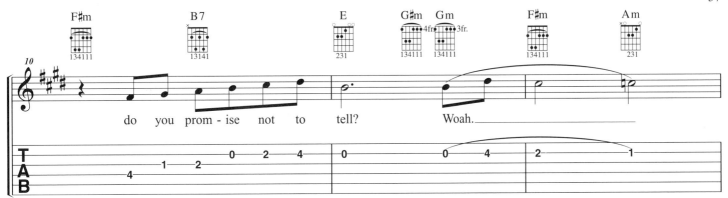

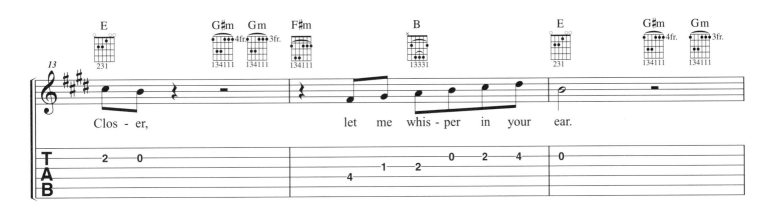

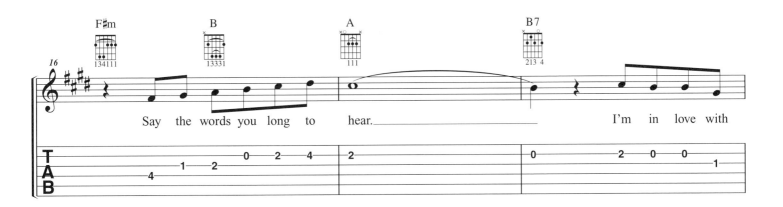

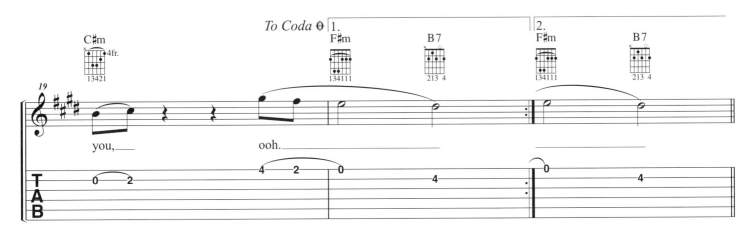

Do You Want to Know a Secret - 3 - 2

38

Bridge:

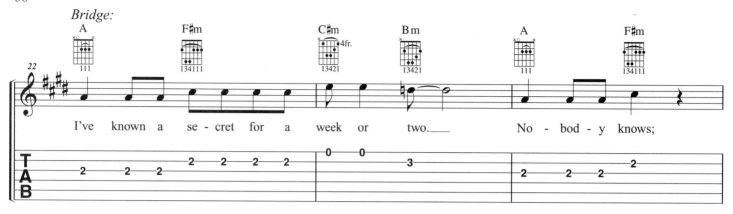

I've known a se - cret for a week or two.___ No - bod - y knows;

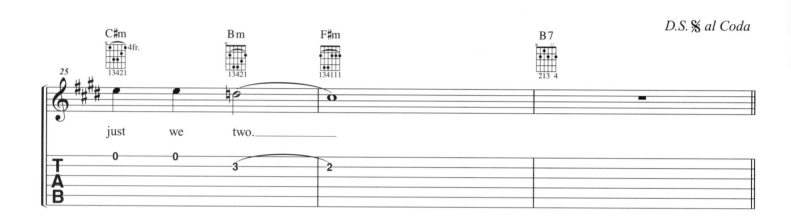

D.S. 𝄋 al Coda

just we two.___

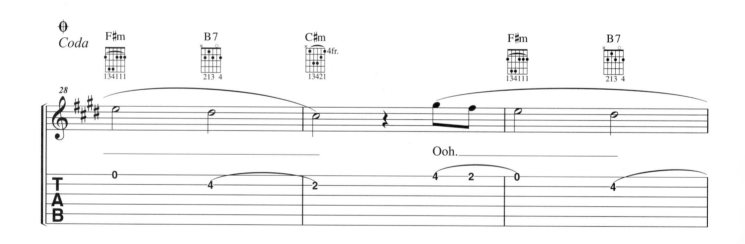

Coda

Ooh.___

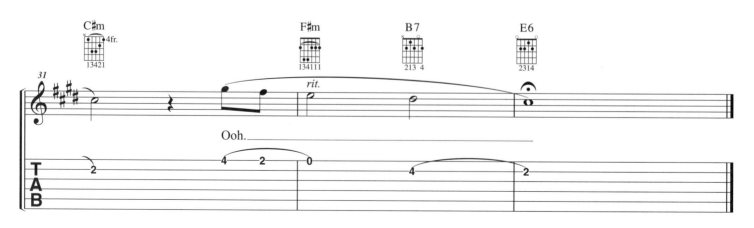

Ooh.___

Do You Want to Know a Secret - 3 - 3

DON'T STOP BELIEVIN'

Use Suggested Strum Pattern #2

Words and Music by
JONATHAN CAIN, NEAL SCHON
and STEVE PERRY

Moderately

42

Verse 3:

Work-in' hard__ to get my fill,__ ev-'ry-bod - y wants a thrill.__

Pay-in' an - y-thing to roll the dice__ just one more__ time.__

Some will win,__ some will lose,__ some are born__ to sing the blues.__

D.S. % al Coda

Oh, the mov-ie nev - er ends,__ it goes on and on__ and on___ and on.__

FEELIN' STRONGER EVERY DAY

Use Suggested Strum Pattern #2
Moderately fast (with a half-time feel) ♩ = 160

Words and Music by
PETER CETERA and JAMES PANKOW

Feelin' Stronger Every Day - 4 - 1

*Sung first time only.

Chorus:

Repeat and fade

GO YOUR OWN WAY

Use Suggested Strum Pattern #2
Moderately ♩ = 136

Words and Music by
LINDSEY BUCKINGHAM

1. Lov - ing you is - n't the right___ thing_ to do.
2. Tell__ me why ev - 'ry-thing turned__ a - round.

How__ can I___ ev - er change things_ that_ I feel?___
Pack - ing up,___ shack - ing up's all__ you wan - na do.___

If__ I could, ba - by, I'd give___ you__ my world.___
If__ I could, ba - by, I'd give___ you__ my world.___

How can I___ when you won't take___ it from_ me?}
O - pen up,___ ev - 'ry-thing's wait - ing for__ you. }

Go Your Own Way - 2 - 1

GOOD TIMES BAD TIMES

Words and Music by
JIMMY PAGE, JOHN PAUL JONES
and JOHN BONHAM

Use Suggested Strum Pattern #7

Moderately ♩ = 95

Good Times Bad Times - 3 - 1

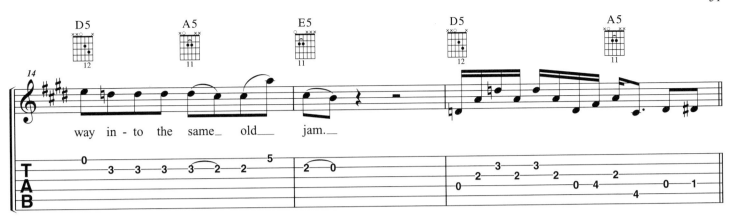

way in - to the same___ old___ jam.___

Chorus:

Good times, bad___ times, you know I've had my share. Well, my wom-an left home for a brown-eyed man, but I

To Coda ✛ Bridge:

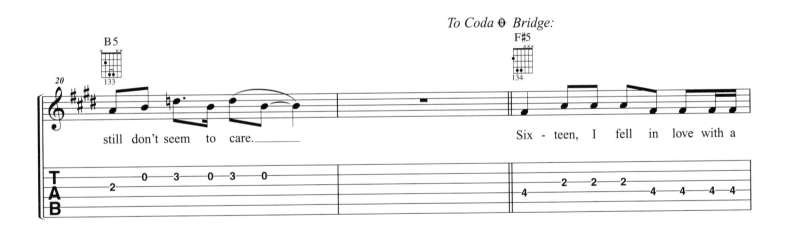

still don't seem to care.___ Six - teen, I fell in love with a

girl as sweet as could be. It on - ly took a cou-ple of days till she was rid of me. She

swore that she would be all mine and love me till the end.__ But when I whis-pered in her ear, I

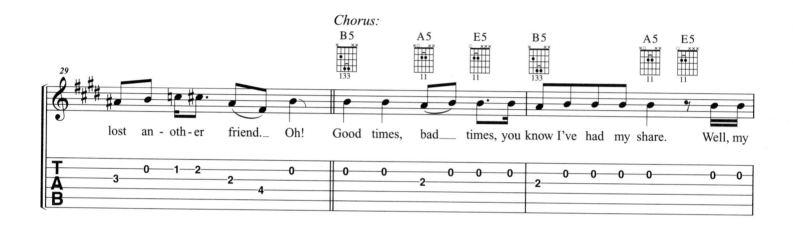

Chorus:

lost an-oth-er friend.__ Oh! Good times, bad__ times, you know I've had my share. Well, my

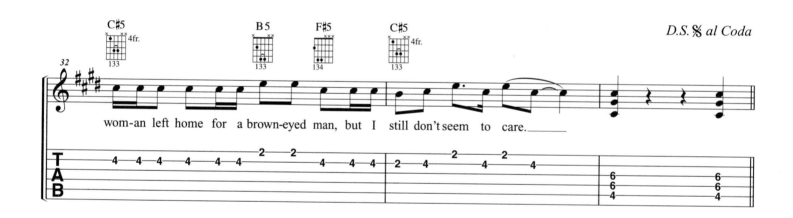

D.S. 𝄋 al Coda

wom-an left home for a brown-eyed man, but I still don't seem to care._____

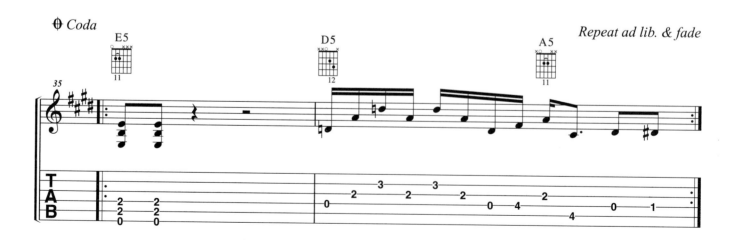

⊕ *Coda*

Repeat ad lib. & fade

HIT ME WITH YOUR BEST SHOT

**Use Suggested Strum Pattern #1
or Rhythm indicated in Intro**

Words and Music by
EDDIE SCHWARTZ

Hit Me with Your Best Shot - 3 - 1

54

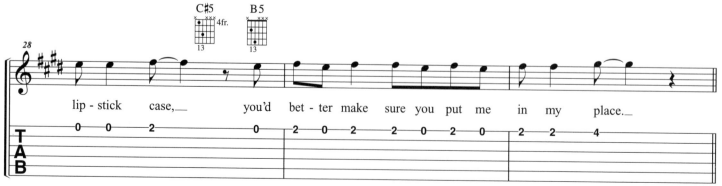

Hit Me with Your Best Shot - 3 - 2

Verse 2:
You come on with a come on, you don't fight fair.
But that's okay, see if I care.
Knock me down, it's all in vain.
I'll get right back on my feet again.
(To Chorus:)

HOLD THE LINE

Use Intro pattern as model for strumming

Words and Music by
DAVID PAICH

Moderately ♩. = 98

1. It's not in the way___ that you hold me,
2.3. It's not in the words___ that you told me,

it's not in the way   you___ say you
it's not in the way   you___ say you're

care.
mine.

It's not in the way   you've_been   treat - ing___ my friends,
It's not in the way   that___ you   came   back___ to me,

it's not in the way   that___ you   stayed till___ the end.⎫
it's not in the way   that___ your   love set___ me free.⎭

It's not in the way you look or the

58

I HEAR YOU KNOCKING

Words and Music by
DAVE BARTHOLOMEW
and PEARL KING

Use Suggested Strum Pattern #1
or use Intro figure as rhythm pattern throughout

Moderately ♩ = 120

Verses 1–3:

went a-way and left me long   time a-go___   and now you're knock-in'
(2.) begged you not to go___ but you   said good-bye___   and now you're tell-ing me
3. See additional lyrics

on my door.___ } I hear you knock-ing   but you can't___ come in.___
all your lies.

I hear you knock-ing,   go back where___ you been.___

To Coda ⊕   1.   2. I

60

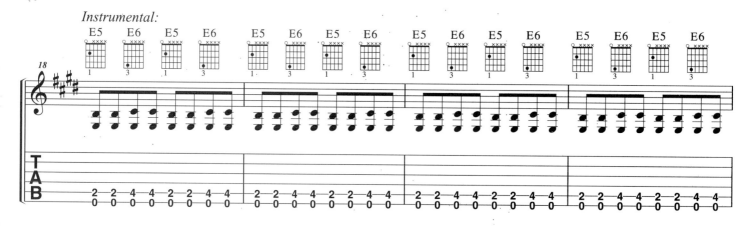

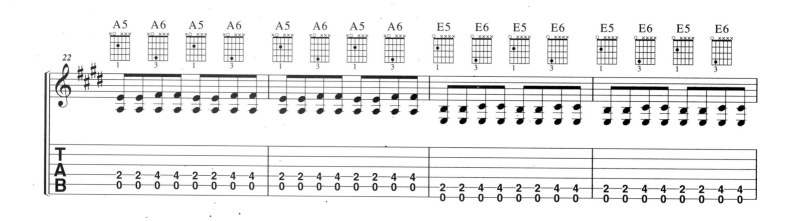

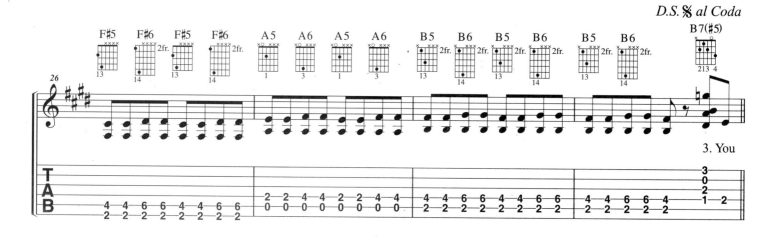

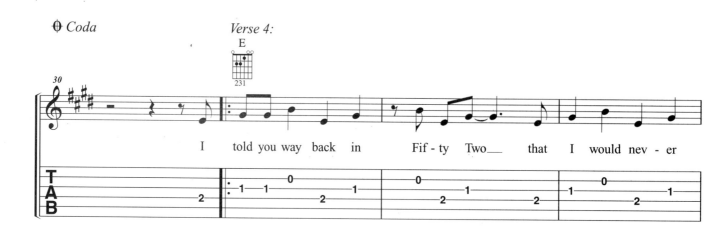

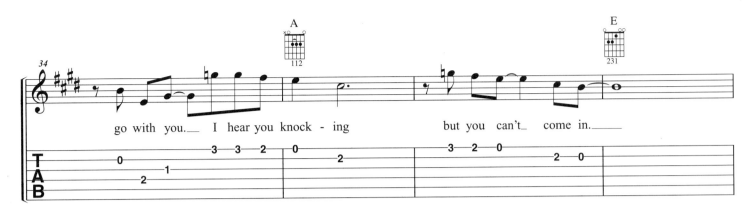

go with you.___ I hear you knock - ing but you can't___ come in.___

I hear you knock - ing, go back where___ you been.___

Repeat ad lib. & fade

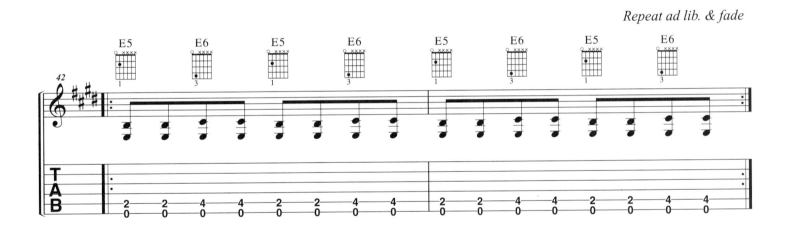

Verse 3:
You better get back to your use to be
'Cause your kind of love ain't good for me.
I hear you knocking but you can't come in.
I hear you knocking, go back where you been.
(To Verse 4:)

HOLD YOUR HEAD UP

Words and Music by
ROD ARGENT and CHRIS WHITE

I SAW HER STANDING THERE

Use Suggested Strum Pattern #1
Moderately fast

Words and Music by
JOHN LENNON and PAUL McCARTNEY

I Saw Her Standing There - 3 - 1

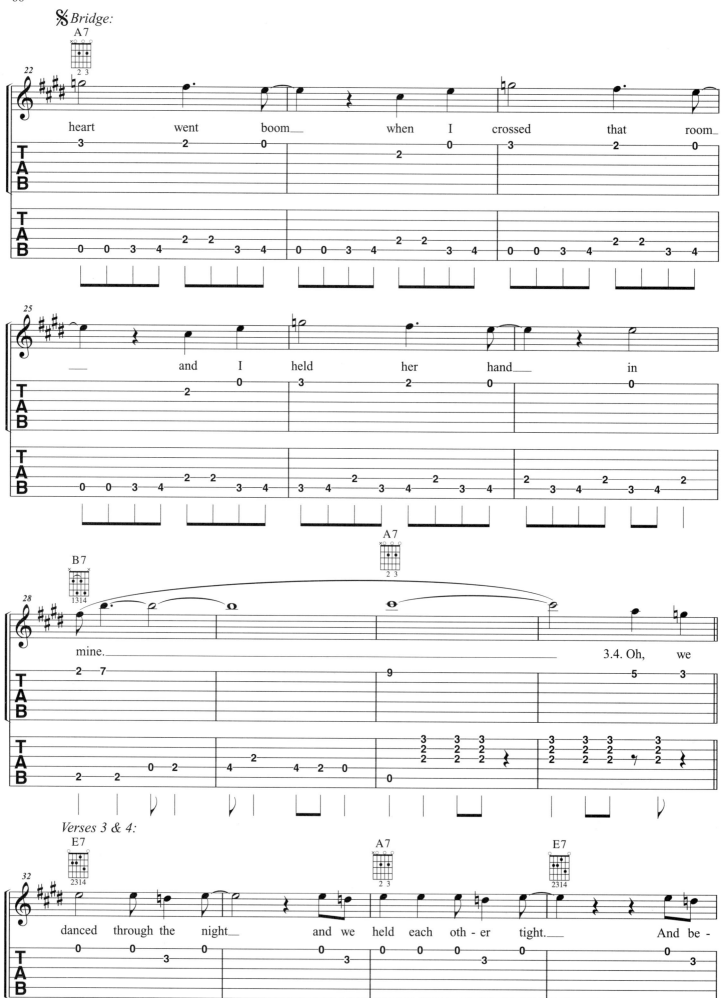

LET'S SPEND THE NIGHT TOGETHER

Use Suggested Strum Pattern #1

Moderately ♩ = 120

Words and Music by
MICK JAGGER and KEITH RICHARDS

70

THE LETTER

Use Suggested Strum Pattern #6

Words and Music by
WAYNE CARSON THOMPSON

The Letter - 2 - 1

LIDO SHUFFLE

Words and Music by
BOZ SCAGGS and DAVID PAICH

Use Suggested Strum Pattern #1 (add a swing/shuffle feel)

Lido Shuffle - 4 - 1

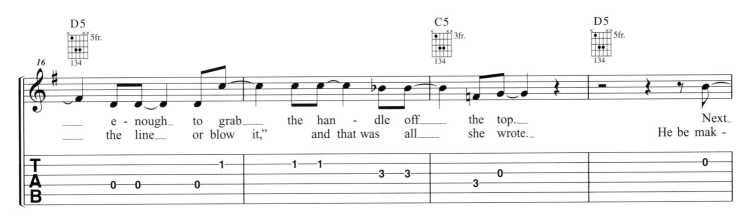

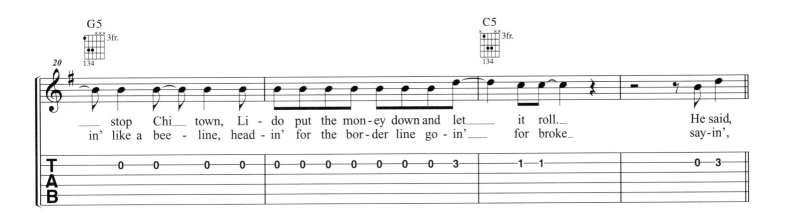

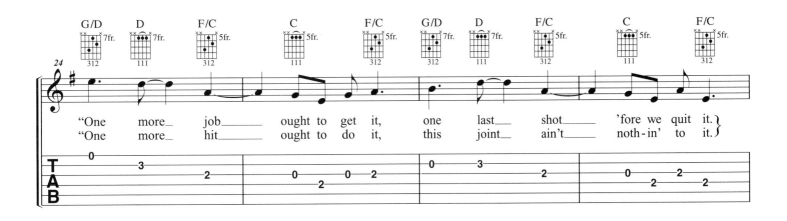

Lido Shuffle - 4 - 2

Chorus:

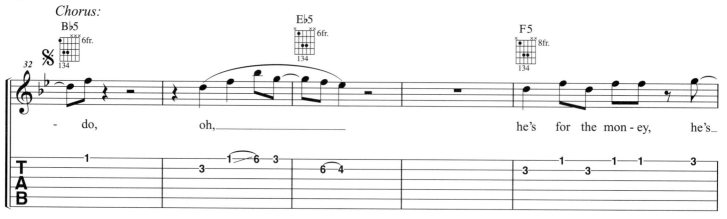

- do, oh,_____ he's for the mon-ey, he's_

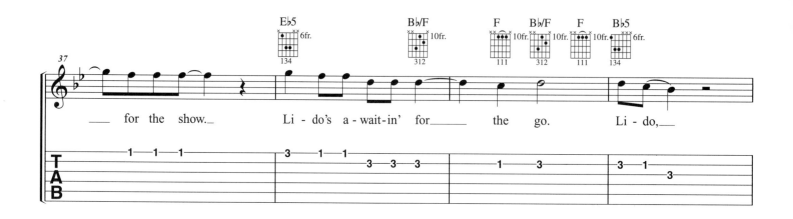

___ for the show.___ Li - do's a - wait-in' for_____ the go. Li - do,___

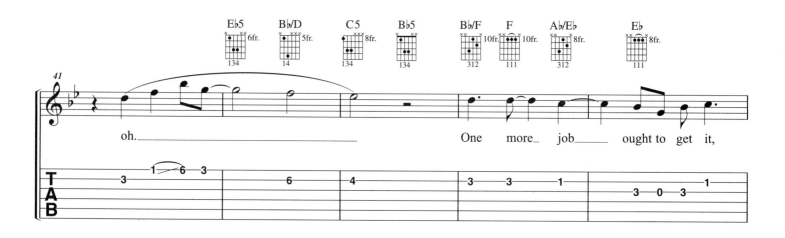

oh._____ One more_ job_____ ought to get it,

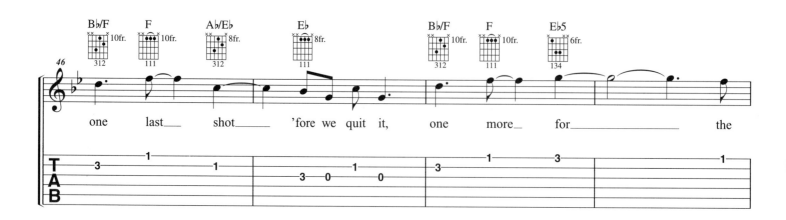

one last___ shot_____ 'fore we quit it, one more_ for_____ the

LIFE IN THE FAST LANE

Use Suggested Strum Pattern #6

Bright rock ♩ = 220 (with a half-time feel)

Intro:

Words and Music by
DON HENLEY, GLENN FREY
and JOE WALSH

Verse:

hard - head - ed man,___ he was bru - tal - ly hand - some,

2.3. See additional lyrics

and she was ter - mi - nal - ly pret - ty. She held him

Life in the Fast Lane - 5 - 1

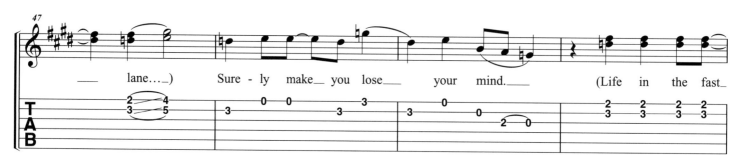

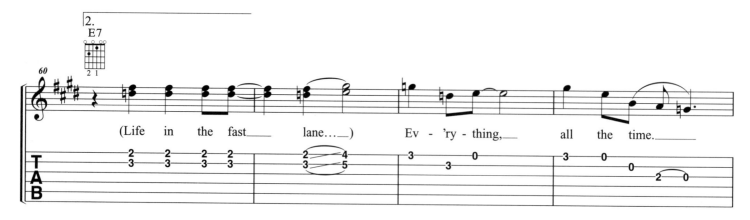

Life in the Fast Lane - 5 - 3

To Coda ✆

(Life in the fast____ lane….__) Ah ha._____

Instrumental:

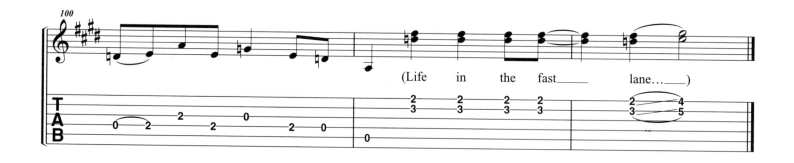

Verse 2:
Eager for action, and hot for the game.
The coming attraction, the drop of a name.
They knew all the right people, they took all the right pills,
They threw outrageous parties, they paid heavenly bills.
There were lines on the mirror, lines on her face.
She pretended not to notice, she was caught up in the race.
Out in the evening, until it was light,
He was too tired to make it, she was too tired to fight about it.
Surely make you lose your mind. Yeah.
(To Chorus:)

Verse 3:
Blowin' and burnin' blinded by thirst,
They didn't see the stop sign, took a turn for the worst.
She said, "listen, baby, you can hear the engine ring,
We've been up and down this highway,
Haven't seen a goddamn thing.
He said, "Call the doctor, I think I'm gonna crash."
"And, doctor say he's comin', but you got to pay him cash."
They went rushin' down that freeway, messin' 'round and got lost,
They didn't care, they were just dying to get off and it was…
(To Chorus:)

LIGHT MY FIRE

Use Suggested Strum Pattern #5

Words and Music by
THE DOORS

LOLA

Moderately bright (with a half-time feel) ♩ = 144

Words and Music by
RAY DAVIES

Intro:

Verses 1 & 2:

met her in a club down in old So - ho___ where you drink cham - pagne and it
I'm___ not the world's most phys - i - cal guy___ but when she squeezed me tight she

tastes just like___ cher - ry co - la, C - O - L - A
near - ly broke my spine, oh my Lo - la, Lo - Lo - Lo Lo -

co - la.
Lo - la.

She walked up to me and she
Well, I'm not___ dumb but I

Lola - 5 - 1

MARRAKESH EXPRESS

Use Suggested Strum Pattern 6
Moderately fast ♩ = 108

Words and Music by
GRAHAM NASH

Marrakesh Express - 5 - 1

94

Verse 3:
Take the train from Casablanca going south,
Blowing smoke rings from the corners of my m-m-m-m-mouth,
Colored cottons hang in the air,
Charming cobras in the square,
Striped djellebas we can wear at home.
Well, let me hear you, now.
(To Chorus:)

ONLY WOMEN BLEED

Use Suggested Strum Pattern #1

Words and Music by
ALICE COOPER and DICK WAGNER

OPEN ARMS

Use Suggested Strum Pattern #9

Words and Music by
JONATHAN CAIN and STEVE PERRY

Gently ♩ = 104

Open Arms - 3 - 1

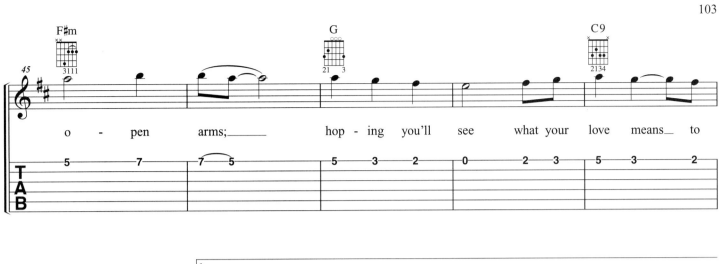

o - pen arms;_____ hop - ing you'll see what your love means__ to

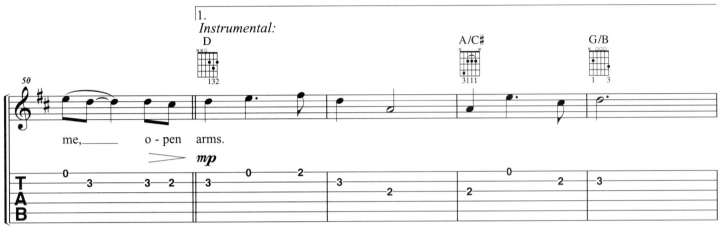

1.
Instrumental:

me,_____ o - pen arms.

mp

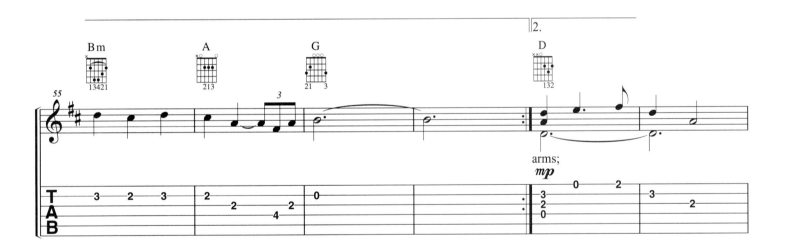

2.

arms;
mp

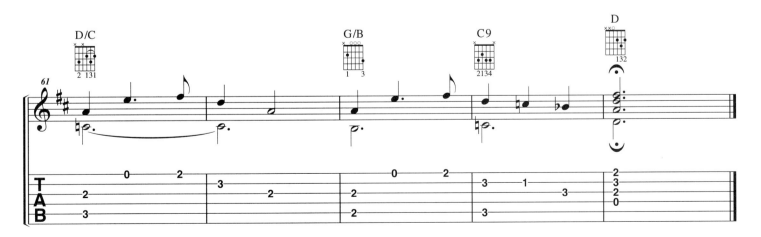

OUR HOUSE

PAINT IT, BLACK

Use Suggested Strum Pattern #1 (all downstrokes)

Words and Music by
MICK JAGGER and KEITH RICHARDS

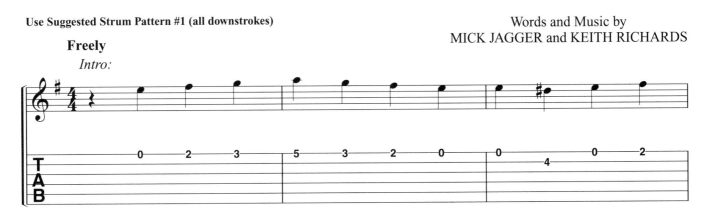

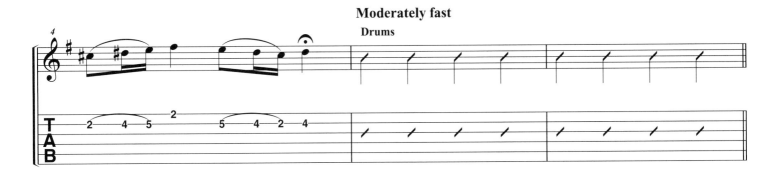

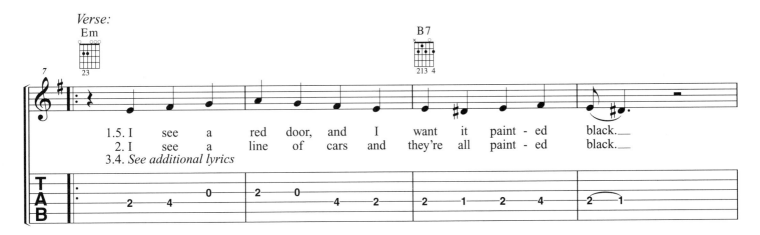

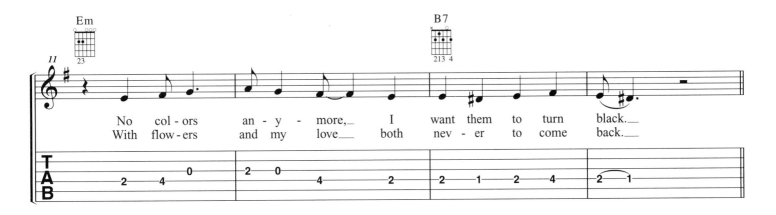

Paint It, Black - 3 - 1

Bridge:

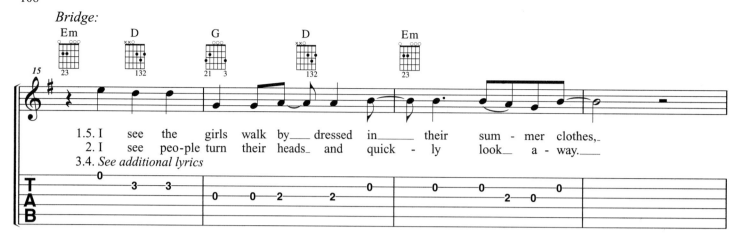

1.5. I see the girls walk by___ dressed in_____ their sum - mer clothes,___
2. I see peo-ple turn their heads_ and quick - ly look__ a - way.
3.4. *See additional lyrics*

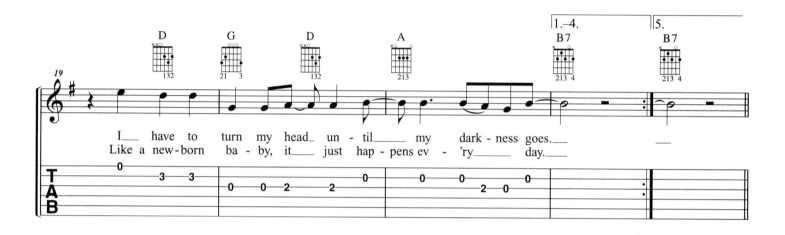

I__ have to turn my head_ un - til___ my dark - ness goes.__
Like a new-born ba - by, it___ just hap - pens ev - 'ry___ day.__

Outro:

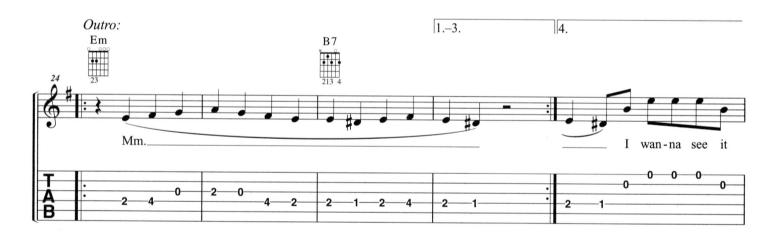

Mm._____ I wan-na see it

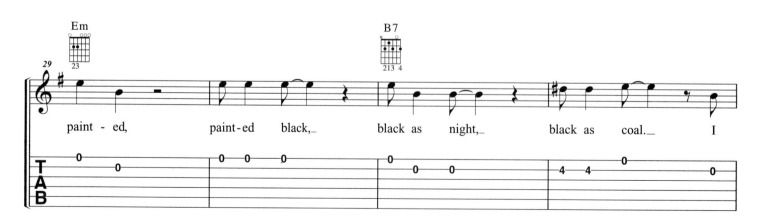

paint - ed, paint-ed black,_ black as night,_ black as coal.__ I

Verse 3:
I look inside myself and see my heart is black.
I see my red door, I must have it painted black.

Bridge 3:
Maybe then I'll fade away and not have to face the facts.
It's not easy facing up when your whole world is black.

Verse 4:
No more will my green sea go turn a deeper blue.
I could not foresee this thing happening to you.

Bridge 4:
If I look hard enough into the setting sun,
My love will laugh with me before the mornin' comes.
(To Verse 5:)

PINBALL WIZARD

Use Suggested Strum Pattern #1
Moderately ♩ = 124

Words and Music by
PETER TOWNSHEND

RIDERS ON THE STORM

Use Suggested Strum Pattern #4
Moderately ♩ = 102

Words and Music by
THE DOORS

Riders on the Storm - 2 - 1

ROCK AND ROLL

Use Suggested Strum Pattern #1
or Intro Figure simile

Words and Music by
JIMMY PAGE, ROBERT PLANT,
JOHN PAUL JONES and JOHN BONHAM

Rock and Roll - 3 - 1

Verse 3:
Oh, it seems so long since we walked in the moonlight,
Making vows that just couldn't work right, ha-ha, yeah.
Open your arms, open your arms, open your arms.
Baby, let my love come running in.
Yes, it's been a long time, been a long time,
Been a long lonely, lonely, lonely, lonely, lonely time.
(To Outro:)

SEPARATE WAYS
(WORLDS APART)

Use Suggested Strum Pattern #5

Moderately ♩ = 132

Words and Music by
JONATHAN CAIN and STEVE PERRY

120

Separate Ways (Worlds Apart) - 5 - 5

(I CAN'T GET NO) SATISFACTION

**Use Suggested Strum Pattern #4
ot Fingerlpicking Pattern #6**

Words and Music by
MICK JAGGER and KEITH RICHARDS

Moderately

Verse 2:
When I'm watchin' my TV,
And a man comes on and tells me
How white my shirts can be,
But he can't be a man 'cause he doesn't smoke
The same cigarettes as me.
I can't get no, oh, no, no, no.
Hey, hey, hey, that's what I say.
(To Chorus:)

Verse 3:
When I'm ridin' 'round the world,
And I'm doin' this and I'm signin' that,
And I'm tryin' to make some girl
Who tells me, baby, better come back maybe next week,
'Cause you see I'm on a losin' streak.
I can't get no, oh, no, no, no.
Hey, hey, hey, that's what I say.
I can't get no…
(To Outro:)

SHE LOVES YOU

Use Suggested Strum Pattern #2

Moderately bright

Words and Music by
JOHN LENNON and PAUL McCARTNEY

She Loves You - 3 - 1

Verse 2:
She said you hurt her so she almost lost her mind.
But now she says she knows you're not the hurting kind.
She said she loves you and you know that can't be bad.
Yes, she loves you and you know you should be glad, oo.
(To Chorus:)

Verse 3:
You know it's up to you, I think it's only fair.
Pride can hurt you too, apologize to her.
Because she loves you and you know that can't be bad.
Yes, she loves you and you know you should be glad, oo.
(To Chorus:)

SPIRIT IN THE SKY

Use Suggested Strum Pattern # 1

Words and Music by
NORMAN GREENBAUM

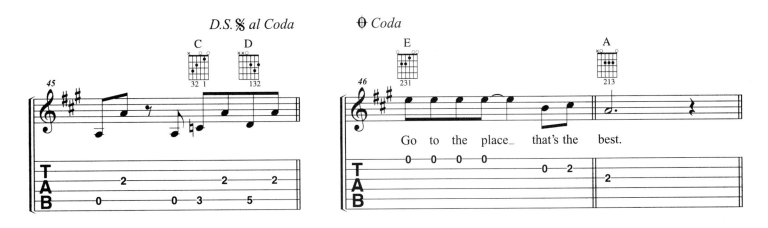

D.S. ℅ al Coda ⊕ *Coda*

Go to the place_ that's the best.

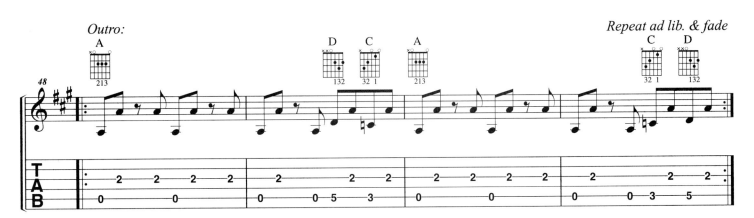

Outro: *Repeat ad lib. & fade*

Verse 2:
Prepare yourself, you know it's a must,
Gotta have a friend in Jesus.
So you know that when you die,
He's gonna recommend you to the spirit in the sky.
Gonna recommend you to the spirit in the sky,
That's where you're gonna go when you die.
When you die and they lay you to rest,
You're gonna go to the place that's the best.

Verse 3:
Never been a sinner, I never sinned,
I got a friend in Jesus.
So you know that when I die,
He's gonna set me up with the spirit in the sky.
Oh, set me up with the spirit in the sky,
That's where I'm gonna go when I die.
When I die and they lay me to rest,
I'm gonna go to the place that's the best.
Go to the place that's the best.

SHE'S NOT THERE

Use Suggested Strum Pattern #6

Moderately ♩ = 132

Words and Music by
ROD ARGENT

She's Not There - 2 - 1

SPACE ODDITY

**Use Suggested Strum Pattern #6
or Continue Intro Pattern Simile**

Moderately slow

Words and Music by
DAVID BOWIE

Play 4 times

STAIRWAY TO HEAVEN

(Excerpt)

Use Suggested Strum Pattern #3

Slowly

Words and Music by
JIMMY PAGE and ROBERT PLANT

Stairway to Heaven (Excerpt) - 3 - 1

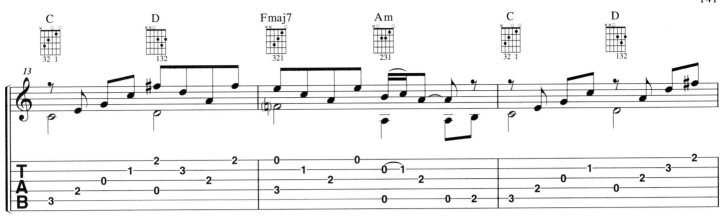

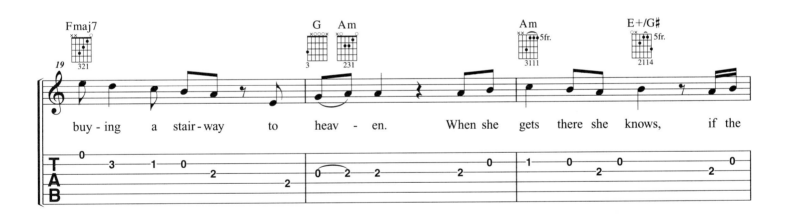

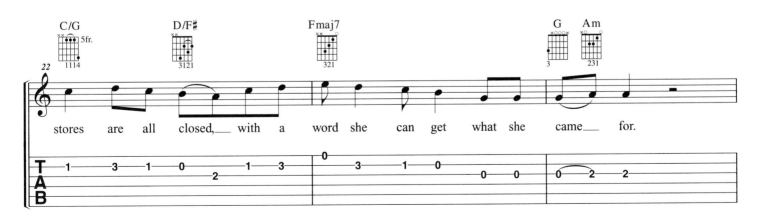

TEACH YOUR CHILDREN

Use Suggested Strum Pattern #6
Moderately bright ♩ = 78

Words and Music by
GRAHAM NASH

TELL HER NO

Use Suggested Strum Pattern #4

Moderately fast ♩ = 134

Words and Music by
ROD ARGENT

Tell Her No - 2 - 1

TIME OF THE SEASON

Use Suggested Strum Pattern #4

Words and Music by
ROD ARGENT

Moderately

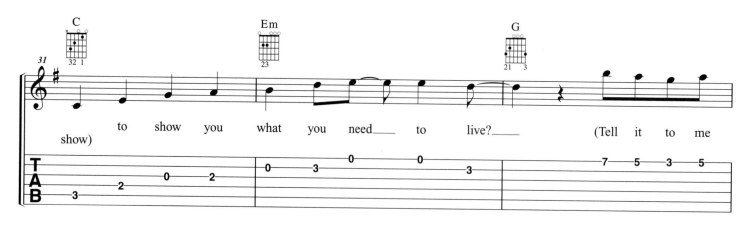

to show you what you need___ to live?___ (Tell it to me
show)

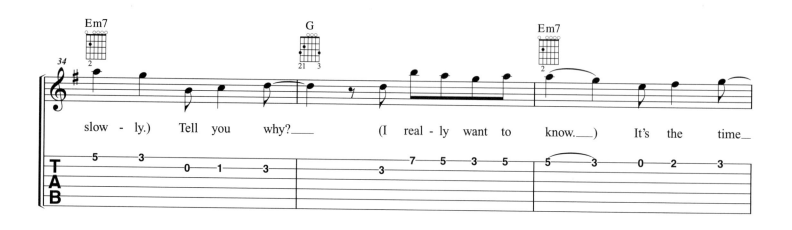

slow - ly.) Tell you why?___ (I real - ly want to know.___) It's the time___

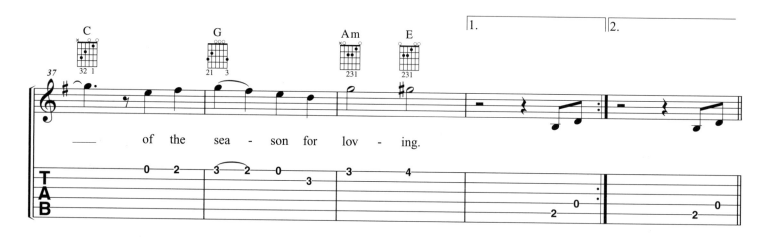

___ of the sea - son for lov - ing.

Outro:
Organ Solo:

Repeat ad lib. & fade

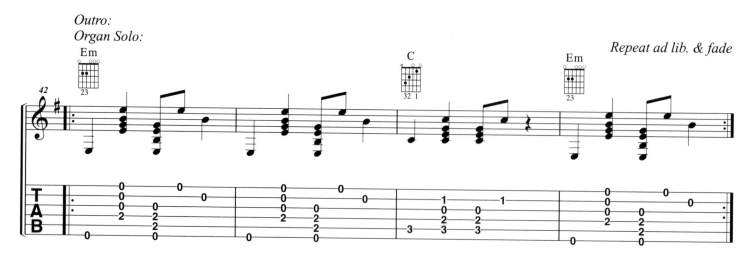

Time of the Season - 3 - 3

WASTED ON THE WAY

Use Suggested Strum Pattern #4

Words and Music by
GRAHAM NASH

*Play a D chord on repeat.

Instrumental:

Wasted on the Way - 3 - 2

Verse 2:
Oh, when you were young, did you question all the answers?
Did you envy all the dancers who had all the nerve?
Look around you now, you must go for what you wanted.
Look at all my friends who did and got what they deserved.
(To Chorus:)

Wasted on the Way - 3 - 3

THE WEIGHT

Use Suggested Strum Pattern #3

Words and Music by
ROBBIE ROBERTSON

The Weight - 3 - 1

The Weight - 3 - 2

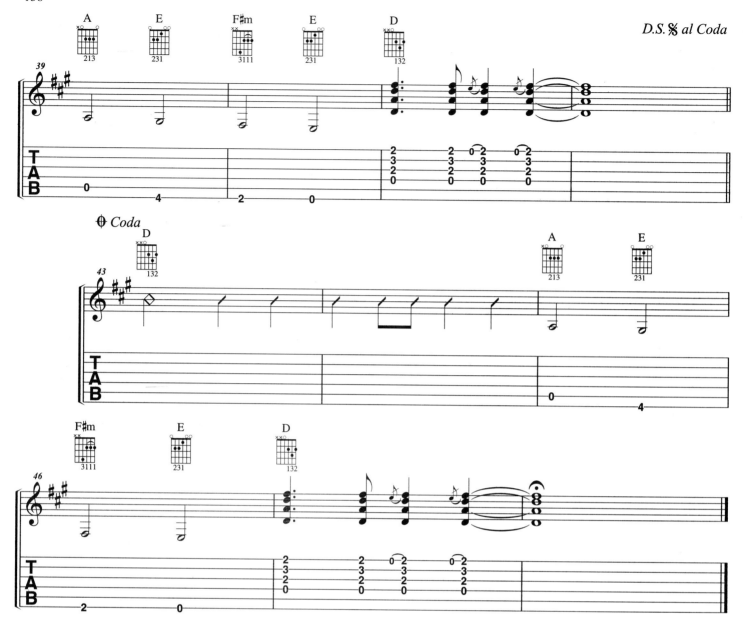

D.S. 𝄉 al Coda

Verse 2:
I picked up my bag, I went lookin' for a place to hide;
When I saw Carmen and the Devil walkin' side by side.
I said, "Hey, Carmen, come on, let's go downtown."
She said, "I gotta go, but my friend can stick around."
(To Chorus:)

Verse 3:
Go down, Miss Moses, there's nothin' you can say,
It's just ol' Luke, and Luke's waitin' on the Judgement Day.
"Well, Luke, my friend, what about young Anna Lee?"
He said, "Do me a favor, son, woncha stay an' keep Anna Lee company?"
(To Chorus:)

Verse 4:
Crazy Chester followed me, and he caught me in the fog.
He said, "I will fix your rack, if you'll take Jack, my dog."
I said, "Wait a minute, Chester, you know I'm a peaceful man."
He said, "That's okay, boy, won't you feed him when you can."
(To Chorus:)

Verse 5:
Catch a cannon ball now, to take me down the line.
My bag is sinkin' low and I do believe it's time.
To get back to Miss Fanny, you know she's the only one
Who sent me here with her regards for everyone.
(To Chorus:)

WHAT A FOOL BELIEVES

Use Suggested Strum Pattern #1

Words and Music by
KENNY LOGGINS and MICHAEL McDONALD

A WHITER SHADE OF PALE

Words and Music by
KEITH REID and GARY BROOKER

Use Suggested Strum Pattern #5

Moderately slow

A Whiter Shade of Pale - 3 - 1

A Whiter Shade of Pale - 3 - 2

Verse 2:
She said, "There is no reason
And the truth is plain to see."
But I wandered through my playing cards,
And would not let her be
One of sixteen vestal virgins
Who were leaving for the coast.
And, although my eyes were open,
They might have just as well've been closed.
And so it was that later,
As the miller told his tale,
That her face, at first just ghostly,
Turned a whiter shade of pale.

WILD HORSES

**Use Suggested Strum Pattern #3
or Continue Intro Pattern Simile**

Words and Music by
MICK JAGGER and KEITH RICHARDS

Moderately slow

Wild Horses - 3 - 1

Verse 2:
I watched you suffer a dull aching pain.
Now you decided to show me the same.
No sweeping exits or offstage lines
Could make me feel bitter, or treat you unkind.
(To Chorus:)

Verse 3:
I know I dreamed you a sin and a lie.
I have my freedom, but I don't have much time.
Faith has been broken, tears must be cried.
Let's do some living after we die.
(To Chorus:)

WOODSTOCK

**Use Suggested Strum Pattern #6
or Fingerpicking Pattern #6**

Words and Music by
JONI MITCHELL

Woodstock - 2 - 1

Verse 2:
Well, then can I walk beside you? I have come to lose the smog.
And I feel as if a cog in something turning.
And maybe it's the time of year, yes, and maybe it's the time of man.
And I don't know who I am but life is for learning.
(To Chorus:)

Verse 3:
By the time we got to Woodstock, we were half a million strong,
And everywhere was a song and a celebration.
And I dreamed I saw the bomber jet planes riding shotgun in the sky,
Turning into butterflies above our nation.
(To Chorus:)

Woodstock - 2 - 2

GUITAR TAB GLOSSARY

TABLATURE EXPLANATION

TAB illustrates the six strings of the guitar.
Notes and chords are indicated by the placement of fret numbers on each string.

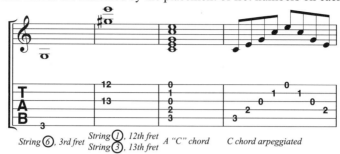

String ⑥, 3rd fret   *String ①, 12th fret*   *A "C" chord*   *C chord arpeggiated*
            String ③, 13th fret

BENDING NOTES

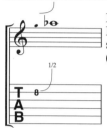
Half Step:
Play the note and bend string one half step (one fret).

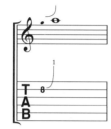
Whole Step:
Play the note and bend string one whole step (two frets).

Slight Bend/ Quarter-Tone Bend:
Play the note and bend string sharp.

Prebend and Release:
Play the already-bent string, then immediately drop it down to the fretted note.

Bend and Release:
Play the note and bend to the next pitch, then release to the original note. Only the first note is attacked.

PICK DIRECTION

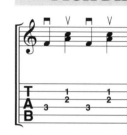
Downstrokes and Upstrokes:
The downstroke is indicated with this symbol (⊓) and the upstroke is indicated with this (∨).

ARTICULATIONS

Hammer On:
Play the lower note, then "hammer" your finger to the higher note. Only the first note is plucked.

Pull Off:
Play the higher note with your first finger already in position on the lower note. Pull your finger off the first note with a strong downward motion that plucks the string—sounding the lower note.

Palm Mute:
The notes are muted (muffled) by placing the palm of the pick hand lightly on the strings, just in front of the bridge.

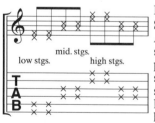
Muted Strings:
A percussive sound is produced by striking the strings while laying the fret hand across them.

Legato Slide:
Play the first note and, keeping pressure applied on the string, slide up to the second note. The diagonal line shows that it is a slide and not a hammer-on or a pull-off.

HARMONICS

Natural Harmonic:
A finger of the fret hand lightly touches the string at the note indicated in the TAB and is plucked by the pick producing a bell-like sound called a harmonic.

RHYTHM SLASHES

Strum Marks/ Rhythm Slashes:
Strum with the indicated rhythm pattern. Strum marks can be located above the staff or within the staff.

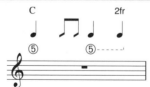
Single Notes with Rhythm Slashes:
Sometimes single notes are incorporated into a strum pattern. The circled number below is the string and the fret number is above.

Artificial Harmonic:
Fret the note at the first TAB number, lightly touch the string at the fret indicated in parens (usually 12 frets higher than the fretted note), then pluck the string with an available finger or your pick.